LOST TRAMWAYS OF ENGLAND
LEEDS EAST

PETER WALLER

GRAFFEG

CONTENTS

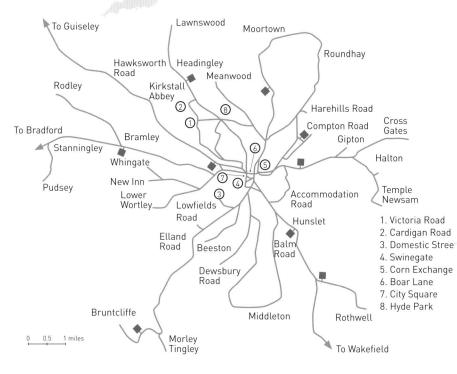

LEEDS EAST

To Guiseley
Lawnswood
Moortown
Roundhay
Hawksworth Road
Headingley
Meanwood
Rodley
Kirkstall Abbey
Harehills Road
Compton Road
Cross Gates
To Bradford
Bramley
Gipton
Stanningley
Halton
Whingate
New Inn
Accommodation Road
Temple Newsam
Pudsey
Lower Wortley
Lowfields Road
Hunslet
Elland Road
Balm Road
Beeston
Dewsbury Road
Middleton
Rothwell
Bruntcliffe
Morley Tingley
To Wakefield

1. Victoria Road
2. Cardigan Road
3. Domestic Street
4. Swinegate
5. Corn Exchange
6. Boar Lane
7. City Square
8. Hyde Park

0   0.5   1 miles

INTRODUCTION

Although there had been street tramways in Britain from the early 1860s in places like Birkenhead and London, it was not until the 1870 Tramways Act that a legislative framework was established for their construction and operation. The Act empowered local authorities to grant licences to companies to operate tramways for a 21-year period. The licensee could construct the tramway itself or the route could be constructed by the local authority and leased as part of the franchise to the operator. Initially, it was expected that private companies would always operate the tramways built; however, in 1883, Huddersfield Corporation in the West Riding of Yorkshire, having constructed a new steam tramway to serve the town, was unable to find a licensee willing to take on operation and so became the first municipal operator of trams within the British Isles.

The 1870 Act imposed a number of restrictions upon the tramway builder and operator; with the benefit of hindsight, it can be seen that these had a negative impact upon tramway development in the United Kingdom and undoubtedly represented one factor in the demise of the tramcar from the 1920s onwards. One of these clauses required the builder and operator of the tramway to maintain the public highway to a distance of 18 inches outside each running line; this effectively made the tramway owner responsible for the upkeep of the road surface on those streets where trams operated. At a time when the condition of the public highway was often poor, the well-built and well-maintained section over which the trams operated became a magnet for other road users. As road traffic increased, so trams – despite the fact that the road had been constructed to accommodate them – were increasingly perceived as a cause of road traffic delays.

The second weakness within the 1870 Act was the so-called 'scrap iron clause'; this permitted the licensor – usually the local authority – to take over the assets (such as the trams) owned by the licensee at asset value – including depreciation – rather than reflecting the value of the business. As a result, tramway licensees became increasingly unwilling to invest in their business as the licence period came towards its end. The Act permitted the termination of the licence after 21 years and every seven years thereafter. For company-owned operations this sword of Damocles meant that the threat of municipalisation was ever present and, even if never exercised, was sufficient to ensure that modernisation might never take place. The classic example here is the tramways of Bristol; operated throughout their career by a company but with the constant threat of takeover by Bristol Corporation, the system survived through until 1941 operating open-top and unvestibuled trams that would not have been out of place on the first electric tramways built at the end of the 19th century, whereas other systems were operating state-of-the-art modern trams by World War II.

This volume is one of a series that cover the tramways of England and is one of two looking at the tramways of Leeds. This volume covers the history of the tramways from the outbreak of war through to the final conversion in November 1959 and the routes that served the eastern half of the city. The other volume covers the history up to the outbreak of World War II and the routes to the west.

The wartime years

The outbreak of World War II in September 1939 had an impact on public transport throughout the country. Petrol rationing was introduced and the blackout was imposed. In order to improve the visibility of the trams during the latter, white bands were painted on the dashes of trams in Leeds whilst protruding parts of the underframe – including the collision fenders – were painted white. To reduce the light from the headlamps, shields were fitted which reduced the visible light to a minimum; these were designed to show either a red or white light depending on the direction of travel.

Inevitably, maintenance and painting also suffered and, during the war, a significant number of trams were painted in an austerity all-khaki livery. Trams so painted included all of the ex-Hull cars acquired in 1942; by 1945, when the last 10 were acquired, the pre-war livery of princess blue had been reinstated.

Another wartime protective measure was the purchase in October 1940 of 22,000 square yards of adhesive cotton netting. This had been purchased to cover the interior of the windows on the trams and buses in order to protect people from the ill effects of glass splinters in the event of blast damage. A number of trams – most notably the 'Middleton Bogies' – were already equipped with toughened safety glass and so did not need the netting whilst most windscreens on both buses and trams were also made of toughened glass and so again did not require protection.

During the course of the war, Leeds suffered – as did most cities – aerial attack by the Luftwaffe. A total of nine raids – the first on 25 August 1940 and the last on 28 August 1942 – inflicted damage on the city. Unlike a number of operators – most notably Bristol and Coventry (where enemy action resulted in the loss of the surviving tram routes) – in Leeds the tramways suffered relatively little damage, although, on 14/15 March 1941, a raid resulted in a number of trams being seriously damaged when bombs hit Swinegate depot. One consequence of this was that sidings were constructed at both Middleton and Temple Newsam to assist with the dispersal of the fleet.

The war also ensured that a number of elderly cars – the majority of those that survived from before World War I – were retained in store in case of possible future use. With the end of the war and with the arrival of the ex-Hull cars (in 1942 and 1945), many of these elderly cars were to be disposed of in the immediate post-war years.

The corporation also undertook some improvements and minor extensions; these included an extension from Balm Road to Belle Isle on 22 July 1940, a short extension of the Dewsbury Road route from Tommy Wass's to Cardinal Drive in 1942 and the doubling of the direct route to Compton Road along Nipper Lane, also in 1942.

The post-war era

At the end of the war the Leeds system extended over some 52 route miles and employed some 450 trams. The pre-war conversion of the routes outside the city's boundaries and the majority of routes with significant sections of single track had improved the financial position and Leeds seemed to be one of the more secure of British tramway operators. There were still a handful of single-track sections remaining but these were not to last long. On 29 August 1946 two routes – the 11 (Nipper Lane, Stanley Road, and Harehills Road) and the 19 (Lower Wortley) – were converted to bus operation, to be followed on

7 December 1947 by the 27 (Victoria Road and Cardigan Road). These losses, however, were countered by improvements elsewhere – such as the new terminal stubs installed on Stainbeck Lane in 1948 and alongside Headingley depot the following year – but much more significant was the completion of the link between the existing termini at Middleton and Balm Road to create a second circular route. However, the opening of the final section – on 28 August 1949 – was to be the last new route opened in the city.

The immediate post-war years represented a period of austerity and the costs involved in maintaining track and overhead were significant. In early 1949 the long section of route beyond Kirkstall Abbey to Hawksworth Road came under examination; it needed relaying, but the cost – estimated at £43,000 – to complete the work was considered prohibitive given that this section carried relatively little traffic; as a result, it was decided on 18 January 1949 to convert the route, the conversion taking place on 3 December 1949.

This was not, however, at this stage, a move towards the wholesale conversion of the system. That the trams still had a future was indicated by the appointment of A. B. Findlay as general manager that same year in succession to Vane Morland. The new manager had previously worked with Glasgow Corporation and had been involved in the development of that operator's modern tramcar fleet from the mid-1930s.

More second-hand trams

Prior to the outbreak of war in 1939, the corporation had acquired three 'HR/2' bogie cars from London Transport; these were to become Leeds Nos 277-79. During the war, the first 32 surplus fully-enclosed four-wheel cars came from Hull Corporation, as did Sunderland Corporation's unique single-deck car No 85 (which became Leeds No 288 initially). With many other British tram operators resuming their abandonment policy once hostilities were over, Leeds took advantage by acquiring additional second-hand cars. The first to arrive were a further 10 fully-enclosed cars in mid-1945 following the conversion of the last Hull route.

The next to be acquired were seven of the 'Pilcher' cars from Manchester Corporation; these fully-enclosed four-wheel cars all dated to the early 1930s and others from the batch were sold to Aberdeen, Edinburgh and Sunderland corporations. These seven were to become Leeds Nos 281-87 (with No 287 being renumbered 280 in 1948). Another operator to withdraw its final trams in 1949 was Southampton Corporation and Leeds acquired a significant number of that operator's distinctively-shaped cars – the roof-line being determined by the necessity of ensuring that they could pass through the medieval Bargate in Southampton (before it was bypassed) – although, in the end, only 11 – Leeds Nos 290-300 – actually entered service.

The arrival of these second-hand cars permitted the withdrawal of most of the final examples of the various batches of trams that Leeds had acquired prior to early 1920s. One pre-World War I car, No 328, was restored to its near original condition (as No 309) for a film in 1948; it was retained thereafter with a view to possible preservation. In the end, however, this was not to be and the tram was scrapped in 1951. No 345 was used as a joinery store after withdrawal in 1948 and was to survive to be preserved; fully restored, it now forms part of the collection of the National Tramway Museum.

The single biggest purchase of second-hand cars was from London Transport. Following the successful test operation of No 2099 – which ran for some time in Leeds still bearing its London Transport fleet number – it was agreed to purchase all of the surviving 'Feltham' type bogie cars as they were withdrawn from service. In all, 90 of the type – 50 ex-Metropolitan Electric Tramways and 40 ex-London United Tramways – reached Leeds; all of the former entered service (as Nos 501-550), as they were the first withdrawn in London, but not all of the latter – allocated fleet numbers 551-90 – did so, with a number being scrapped in Leeds without entering service and a number being stored for some time before finally appearing during 1955 and 1956. In addition to these cars, Leeds also acquired the unique London Transport No 1; this had been built by the London County Council as a prototype in 1932 and was to become Leeds No 301. The arrival of the ex-London cars was to have a further influence in that it was decided that the future livery for the tram fleet would be red rather than the blue that had been adopted earlier. At the same time, it was agreed that the predominant colour for the bus fleet would be green; this was to remain until the final disappearance of Leeds City Transport in April 1974.

Grand plans for the future

There were a number of factors that made trams seem less attractive as a means of transport; one of these was the increased level of transport generally and the congestion that arose as a result. With their fixed routes and – historically – the way that passengers had to walk out to the centre of the road to board them, trams were considered to add to the problems of congestion and delay.

On the continent thoughts were turning to the possibility of constructing tram subways as a means of segregating types of traffic. There was already an existing tram subway in Britain – the Kingsway subway in London – which linked the Embankment with Southampton Row and which had been modernised in the early 1930s to accommodate double-deck trams.

Towards the end of the war, with post-war reconstruction in mind, the corporation started to develop plans that would have seen tramcars eliminated from the surface in the centre of the city, with a network of tram subways, operated with modern single-deck trams, replacing them. The purchase of Sunderland No 85 in 1944 was to enable a prototype single-deck subway car to be constructed.

Although the austerity of the immediate post-war period meant that the project was not progressed, however, despite no progress being made on the subway plans, the corporation did complete the construction of three experimental single-deck cars – Nos 600-02 – during 1953 and 1954. No 600 was the ex-Sunderland car rebuilt but the other two were wholly new, with bodies supplied by the local manufacturer Charles H. Roe – the only tram bodies constructed by the company – with bogies supplied by EMB or Maley & Taunton. In addition, No 602 was equipped with variable automatic multinotch brakes and acceleration control (VAMBAC) electrical equipment manufactured by Crompton-Parkinson; this made it one of the technically most advanced trams ever to operate in Britain.

However, by the time that these new trams were completed the future of the Leeds system was in doubt and the three cars were all destined for a relatively short life.

Politics intervene

The major turning point in the history of the Leeds system was the local election of 1953. The council had been run by the Conservatives for the previous two years and, under the influence of Councillors Donald Cowling and Bertrand Mather, the tramways had undergone some improvements. The Conservatives went into the election as the proponents of tramway retention; however, the Labour and Liberal parties both favoured conversion. When, following the vote, the Labour Party took control, the tramway's fate was sealed.

One factor in this was the deterioration in the transport department's finances and, at a meeting of the new council on 14 June 1953, it was decided to covert two routes – the 4 to Kirkstall Abbey and the 14 to Half Mile Lane – to bus operation as both were significant loss makers. The 14 was converted on 4 October 1953; a month later, on 16 November, the council agreed that the policy was to see all of the surviving tram routes converted to bus operation over a period of 10 years.

The conversion era

With the new policy firmly in place, two routes were to be converted to bus operation during 1954. These were the 4 to Kirkstall Abbey and the 10 to Compton Road, both of which were converted on 3 April. The replacement bus service – the 4 – linked Kirkstall Abbey with Compton Road. Following the conversion of route 4, the section of track leading to Kirkstall Road Works remained operational in order to permit tram access to the workshops; this was to survive until November 1957. Thereafter, all repair work was undertaken at Swinegate depot, with any trucks requiring repair being transferred to Kirkstall Road by road. A further short section to be abandoned during 1954 without replacement was the part of route 8 beyond Elland Road football ground to the greyhound stadium; this section was only operated when a race meeting at the stadium was being held.

The arrival of the 'Felthams' had seen the elimination of a number of older types of car. The last of the ex-Hull and ex-Southampton cars had all been taken out of service by the end of 1951 whilst withdrawals of the 'Chamberlain' cars – Nos 1-150 and 411-45 – had also commenced. Also withdrawn as a result of the introduction of the 'Felthams' were the majority of the corporation-built trams Nos 340-410, the last survivors being withdrawn by the end of 1954; No 399 was used as a works shunter following withdrawal and was to be preserved as the only example of the 'Beeston Air Brakes' to survive. It is now fully restored at the National Tramway Museum. The conversions of 1954 were also to see the demise of the last of the ex-Manchester cars.

The first route to be withdrawn during 1955 was the 11 to Gipton on 23 April. This was followed on 25 June by the conversion of route 8 to Elland Road; the final football specials to the siding on Lowfields Road had operated earlier (on 3 May). The track along Elland Road to the siding into the yard off Lowfields Road was retained, however, until 26 October 1957 as the yard was used for the scrapping of redundant tramcars. Also converted on 25 June was route 6 to Meanwood. The final conversion of this year was on 19 November, when the Beeston service – the 5 – succumbed. The demise on the previous day of the Beeston to Harehills service – which had been reduced to a peak hours only service on Mondays to Fridays from 25 June 1955 – resulted in the elimination of the final trams from Vicar Lane.

The first routes to succumb during 1956 were the 27 – from Belle Isle to Hyde Park – and the 1 – to Lawnswood – that were converted on 2 March

and 3 March respectively. This was followed on 21 July by the conversion of the two routes that operated along Tong Road: the 15 to Whingate and the 16 to New Inn. Prior to 1 October 1950, when the Whingate service had been renumbered route 15, the 16 had been applied to both routes.

However, towards the end of 1956, with Britain embroiled in the Suez Crisis and with fuel rationing briefly reintroduced, the corporation took advantage of the still extant track along Elland Road to reintroduce football specials. These first operated on 8 December 1956 and linked the football ground with Sovereign Street; as conditions improved during early 1957, these were to be withdrawn on 16 March.

The last two years

By the start of 1957 the Leeds system had contracted effectively to the two main circular routes – Roundhay and Middleton – plus the routes off the York Road (to Cross Gates, Halton and Temple Newsam) and the short routes to Dewsbury Road and to Hunslet. These were operated primarily by 'Horsfields' and 'Felthams', although a handful of non-standard types – including the three single-deck cars (Nos

600-02) and the ex-London No 301 – were still operational. The last of the 'Chamberlain' cars had been withdrawn by the end of 1956. By the end of 1957 all of the non-standard cars had also been withdrawn (including the 'Middleton Bogies' and the only four-wheel car to be completed after World War II), leaving passenger services exclusively to the surviving 'Horsfields' and 'Felthams'.

After the withdrawals in July 1956 there was to be a gap of more than a year before the next route conversions. On 28 September 1957 two routes – the 2 to Moortown (via Chapeltown) and the 9 to Dewsbury Road – were replaced. Following the conversion of the Lawnswood service, with which some of the Roundhay circle cars had been linked, on 4 March 1956, the trams that had previously operated to Lawnswood now ran through to Dewsbury Road. The conversion of the 2 saw the demise of the western half of the Roundhay circle; the surviving service – route 3 – was extended to terminate along Street Lane in Moortown itself. This service was the last to use Briggate at North Street.

There were to be no conversions during 1958 and the system's final year dawned on 1 January 1959 with some 120 trams still operational; of these about 70 were 'Horsfields' and the remainder were 'Felthams'.

The first conversions of the year took place on 28 March with the demise of the two Middleton circle routes – the 12 and the 26 – which resulted in the abandonment of the final extension only a decade after its opening. Also converted on this day was the 3 – the remaining section of the Roundhay circle – which resulted in the reintroduction of the circular service, albeit now operated by bus. The southern section of the route – as far as the siding of route 17 (a peak hours only service) at Harehills Lane – remained operational; the trams on the 17, which had been previously linked with the Middleton circle, were to operate only as far as Corn Exchange until their final conversion.

The penultimate conversion occurred on 18 April when the short route to Hunslet – the 25 – succumbed. This had once been part of the long route through to Rothwell and Wakefield. Beyond the city boundary, the track had been controlled by the Yorkshire (West Riding) Electric Tramways Ltd, although the corporation had operated through to Rothwell until the company converted its tramways to bus operation on 31 May 1932. The survival of the Hunslet service until 1959 was something of an anachronism but was largely the result of a lack of a suitable turning circle for the replacement bus service.

The end of the Leeds system was to come on 7 November 1959 when the remaining four routes – the 17 to Harehills Lane, the 18 to Cross Gates, the 20 to Halton and the 22 to Temple Newsam – were converted. The last car in public service was 'Horsfield' No 181, which had been the last outbound car to Cross Gates at 4.39pm and which returned to the Corn Exchange at 5.30pm. At 6.15pm the final closure procession, which comprised 10 'Horsfield' cars (including Nos 160 – the official last car – and 178 suitably decorated), departed; five of the trams headed to Cross Gates and five to Temple Newsam. The two batches then headed back to Swinegate with the last arriving back at 7.16pm. After almost 70 years, the last electric trams had officially operated.

The process of dismantling the surviving trams in Swinegate then proceeded apace. Fortunately, a significant number of Leeds trams were to be preserved. Apart from Nos 345 and 399, plus Hull No 132 (Leeds No 446), already mentioned,

'Horsfield' No 180 and two of the single-deck cars – Nos 600 and 602 – are now at the National Tramway Museum along with a works car (No 2). No 301 is also at Crich and, at the time of writing, is undergoing a major restoration project that will see it restored to its original London County Council condition as No 1. Two of the ex-Metropolitan Electric Tramways 'Feltham' cars – London Transport Nos 2085 (Leeds No 526) and 2099 (Leeds No 500) – survive as well; the former in the USA and the latter as part of the London Transport Museum collection. Also preserved, and now based on the Heaton Park Tramway, is the ex-Hull works car No 96 (Leeds No 6), which has been restored as a single-deck passenger car. Unfortunately, a number of other trams – including two 'Horsfields' (Nos 160 and 202), as well as ex-London United Tramways 'Feltham' London No 2138 (Leeds 554; renumbered 517) and the third single-deck car (No 601) – were also preserved but were to suffer vandalism damage on the Middleton Railway and were subsequently scrapped.

A note on the photographs

The majority of the illustrations in this book have been drawn from the collection of the Online Transport Archive, a UK-registered charity that was set up to accommodate collections put together by transport enthusiasts who wished to see their precious images secured for the long-term. Further information about the archive can be found at: www.onlinetransportarchive.org or email secretary@onlinetransportarchive.org.

DEPOTS

The corporation's main depot and workshop was situated on Kirkstall Road and, in this view, two 'Horsfields' – Nos 231 and 234 – are pictured alongside each other on 10 June 1950. The former has just been equipped with the new – simpler – destination display whilst the latter still retains its original three-line display. The depot and works at Kirkstall Road dated originally to its official opening on 29 July 1897, although it ceased to be a running shed for trams in 1931. It continued to handle the maintenance and repainting of trams until 8 November 1957, served by the remnant of the route to Kirkstall Abbey following that service's conversion on 3 April 1954, when all tram work was transferred to Swinegate for the last two years of operation.

The tram depot at Headingly originally dated to 1874 when it initially accommodated the horse trams of the Leeds Tramways Co. Used for steam trams between 1884 and 1892, the first electric trams were housed in late 1900. The original depot, much modified over the years, was demolished in 1934 and replaced by the structure illustrated in this view; the rebuilt depot opened on 30 June 1935. It ceased to be a tram depot on 3 April 1954 and was incorporated into an enlarged bus garage. It has subsequently been demolished and the site redeveloped for housing. Pictured outside the depot is No 277; this was the first of three ex-London Transport 'HR/2' bogie cars acquired by the corporation in 1939. The tram was built originally in 1930 by Hurst Nelson of Motherwell on bogies supplied by the Electro-Mechanical Brake Co Ltd of West Bromwich. The tram was the first of the trio to be withdrawn, on 23 October 1956, when it was damaged in a collision with 'Horsfield' No 171 at Oakwood.

Pictured on the single track on Torre Road, which gave access to the depot, is 'Feltham' No 516. The most modern of the tram depots that served the corporation, Torre Road comprised a main shed, seen behind the tram, which was used to house both buses (to the west) and trams (to the east), with a second depot – 'Top Shed' – that was situated to the south of the main building. The new depot was officially opened on 8 April 1937. It continued to accommodate trams until 19 November 1955 and was then used to house buses only until its final closure in 1996. The main shed was demolished that year, with the 'Top Shed' following two years later. No 516 – ex-London Transport No 2080 – was to survive in service until March 1957.

Pictured standing at the Sovereign Street entrance to Swinegate depot during an enthusiasts' tour is 'Horsfield' No 189 (previously No 180 and eventually preserved). Located to the south of New station, the first phase of Swinegate depot with its storage sidings beneath the railway arches was opened on 13 October 1914. The following month, however, the building was requisitioned by the military for use during World War I and was not to be restored as a tram depot until 26 September 1919. The depot was extended between 1927 and 1931, when the section of the depot illustrated here was completed; the site had previously been occupied by the corporation's Gas Department works. With the cessation of overhauls at Kirkstall Road in late 1957, Swinegate undertook all routine maintenance work on the tram fleet and was also the last of the corporation's operational tram depots, this work ceasing with the final abandonment of the system on 7 November 1959. For the next few months, the final trams were scrapped at Swinegate. The building, used thereafter as a bus depot, has been demolished and the site redeveloped.

In the background is Stores Car No 6; this was acquired from Hull Corporation, alongside a number of passenger cars, in 1942. It had originally been new in 1901 as No 96 and had been converted into a single-deck works car in 1933. No 6 was preserved following the final abandonment and is now restored as a single-deck passenger car on the Heaton Park tramway, near Manchester. The works cars were generally painted grey, as shown by both of the trams illustrated, whilst the twin headlights were designed for use on the extensive reservations on the system. The site of the yard is now unrecognisable, having been fully redeveloped.

In addition to its operational depots, the corporation also possessed a permanent way yard to the south of Swinegate depot and Sovereign Street. This was equipped with wharfs on the north side of the River Aire, which permitted material – such as setts – to be delivered by water.

Pictured in the yard in April 1954 are two of the significant number of works cars operated by the corporation. Closest to the camera is Stores Car No 2; this had been converted from passenger car No 73A (originally No 73 of 1904) in 1937.

Like all transport operators, the corporation had to take measures to cater for the exigencies of the blackout and the threat of attack by the Luftwaffe. Pictured alongside snowbroom No 3 is No 335 on 13 May 1942. This view shows to good effect some of the necessary precautions – the anti-blast fabric on the windows, the white painted fenders, the white strip on the dashes and the headlamp shields – that were a feature of the tram fleet during World War II. No 335 was one of the trams that had been acquired by the corporation prior to 1915 that were effectively stored for much of the war – No 335 last operated in about 1941 – in case they were required to replace trams damaged or destroyed by enemy action. As such, they survived until after the war; No 335 was scrapped in November 1945.

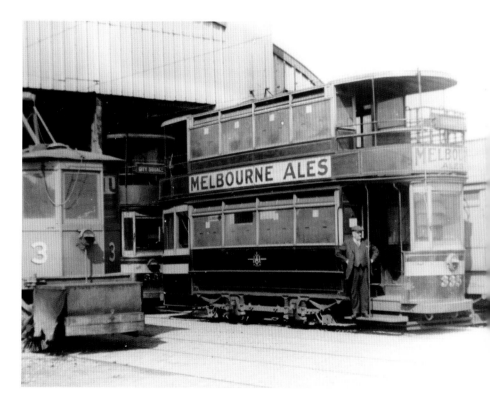

SOUTH FROM THE STATION

In the period between 1946 and 1949 the corporation put into service seven cars – 281-87 originally (with No 287 subsequently being renumbered 280) – that were acquired second-hand from Manchester Corporation. The 'Pilcher' cars, named after the Manchester general manager Stuart Pilcher, were the last new trams acquired by that operator and were new between 1930 and 1932. All were fitted with Peckham P35 trucks but the Leeds cars were destined for a relatively short life, all being withdrawn between 1952 and 1954. Here No 284, originally Manchester No 144, is seen turning from Swinegate into Briggate on 21 August 1949. More than 70 years on, although the names may have changed – the Golden Lion Hotel is now the Cosmopolitan, for example – the buildings illustrated here are largely unchanged; the most dramatic alteration – other than the loss of the trams – is the electrification of the main railway line to the east of Leeds City station.

Heading south from the intersection of Briggate and Swinegate, trams on services towards Hunslet, Middleton, Beeston and Elland Road all made use of Bridge End to pass over the River Aire and, on 21 August 1949, 'Chamberlain' No 146 in blue livery is pictured heading south with a service on route 9 towards Beeston. Although the block immediately adjacent to the tram is still extant – albeit modernised – those buildings visible on the north bank of the Aire have been redeveloped and replaced by modern apartment blocks. The last service to use the section over Bridge End was the route to Hunslet, which was converted to bus operation on 18 April 1959.

DEWSBURY ROAD

With public house The Tommy Wass in the background, which is situated at the junction of Dewsbury Road and Old Lane, 'Chamberlain' No 22 is seen at the original terminus of the route prior to heading back towards the city centre. In 1935 powers were obtained to extend the tramway further westwards; however, work was not progressed and, despite the powers being renewed during the war, only a short extension – opened in 1941 – was completed to Cardinal Drive. During the wartime blackout there had been a number of accidents, with vehicles running into stationary trams at the original terminus and the extension meant that trams terminating no longer blocked the busy road junction. The pub's unusual name derives from the name of the farmer (and landlord) of Bridge Farm, which became the public house, during the 19th century. Although undated, this view dates to the early 1950s when inbound cars headed on route 10 towards Compton Road; the Compton Road section was converted to bus operation on 3 April 1957. The Dewsbury Road section, which was one of the most profitable on the system, was itself converted to bus operation on 28 September 1957. No 22 was to retain its problematic Pivotal truck through until withdrawal, as shown to good effect in this view, unlike a number of others that received replacement P35 trucks after 1945. New in January 1927, it was finally withdrawn in April 1953.

MIDDLETON ROUTE

The Middleton route was first opened from Dewsbury Road to Middleton Arms on 10 November 1925. One of the first features that the new tramway encountered was the railway overbridge that carried the ex-Great Northern Railway freight-only line from Beeston Junction, on the line towards Wakefield, to Hunslet. In this April 1954 view the last of the English Electric-built 'Middleton Bogies' – No 271 – is pictured heading northbound under the railway bridge with an inbound service on route 12. The Middleton route, with its long section of reserved track, was one of the finest high-speed routes in the country. The railway line, which opened originally on 3 July 1899, was closed completely in two stages: from Parkside Junction (where it connected into the private Middleton Railway) to Hunslet on 3 January 1966 and from Parkside Junction

westwards to Beeston Junction on 3 July 1967. Subsequently, the bridge illustrated here was demolished. Today, this area has been transformed through the construction of the M621 as well as commercial and residential development.

Much of the route through to Middleton opened in 1925 was on a private right of way through Middleton Woods and, in April 1954, the first of the production batch of 'Horsfield' cars – No 155 – is pictured on this section. The notice affixed to the traction column warns that it is dangerous to walk on this tramway and that trespassers will be prosecuted. Middleton Woods still exist – albeit now without trams – and so pedestrians are presumably now safe to walk where trams once operated. The services that operated over the Middleton circle were converted to bus operation on 28 March 1959.

On 26 November 1927 the existing route to Middleton was extended from the Middleton Arms to Lingwell Road; this was to be the terminus of the route for two decades, except for a short 150-yard extension opened in 1941 as part of the corporation's plans for the dispersal of the fleet in case of enemy action destroying its depots. Pictured at the terminus is one of the Brush-built 'Middleton Bogies' – No 256 – awaiting departure with a service towards Swinegate. Note the twin headlamps, which were required for operation over the Middleton Light Railway, and the triangle adjacent to the fleet number, which indicated that air brakes were fitted. Work started after the war in completing the Middleton loop, with the system's final major extension being completed in three phases: from Belle Isle Circus to Belle Isle (Middleton Road) on 24 February 1946; thence to Belle Isle (Ring Road) on 6 March 1949; and, finally, from there to Lingwell Road on 28 August 1949.

Following the completion of the new extension from Lingwell Road to Belle Isle, the original terminus at Lingwell Road was provided with a third track and siding in order that those trams terminating there could stand at the terminus without causing delays to through trams on the circular route. Pictured at the revised terminus on 10 June 1950 is 'Middleton Bogie' No 261 whilst in the distance 'Horsfield' No 190 is heading towards Middleton Woods with an inbound service on route 26.

The number of tramway extensions built in Britain during the post-war years was extremely small; one of the most significant was that constructed in Leeds to link the existing termini at Middleton and Balm Road. The route had been extended from Balm Road to Middleton Road in 1946. Work on the construction of the final mile-long line commenced in 1948. Some of the track used was second-hand, salvaged from the closed routes on Victoria Street and Beckett Street, on a concrete foundation; this view records work in progress on the extension. The extension was finally opened in two stages on 6 March 1949 and 28 August 1949 (when cars commenced to operate the circular route).

Pictured at the Belle Isle (Ring Road) terminus of route 27 is 'Chamberlain' No 86. The section from Belle Isle (Circus) to this point opened on 6 March 1949. Beyond the tram can be seen the track through to Middleton. Following the conversion of the Cardigan Road service on 7 December 1947, trams terminated at a short spur on Victoria Road, which was known as Hyde Park. With the closure of the spur on 15 August 1952, route 27 terminated at a crossover on the city side of Hyde Park. The Belle Isle to Hyde Park service was converted to bus operation on 2 March 1956.

The relatively short route to Balm Road, opened on 1 June 1905, left the Hunslet route to head along Waterloo Road before terminating at the junction of Balm Road and Moor Road. The outermost section – the last quarter mile – was single track with a passing loop until the line was doubled during 1940 contemporaneously with the extension of the route to Belle Isle (Circle), which opened on 22 July 1940 (one of a number of enhancements made to the Leeds network during the war). Pictured at the original terminus prior to the war is 'Chamberlain' No 146.

Hunslet Lane was used by trams on services from Hunslet (outbound services used Great Wilson Street to access Hunslet Road) as well as to and from Middleton via Balm Road. Here 'Horsfield' No 189 is seen heading southbound; in the distance, visible above the boy clambering onto the rear platform, can be seen a second tram; this is on Meadow Lane, which was used latterly by services to and from Middleton via Moor Road, Dewsbury Road and Beeston. The 'Horsfields', which was the nickname given to the type by enthusiasts, were officially known as 'Showboats'. The photographer records No 189 as being on a tour; judging by the crowded platform and eager faces peering through windows, that would appear to be the case. No 189 had originally been No 180; withdrawn in 1957 as a source of spare parts, it was to re-enter service in April 1958 after an accident the previous month when the original No 189 was written off. As No 189, the tram survived until the final closure of the system and was subsequently preserved. It is now part of the National Tramway Museum collection at Crich, restored to its original number. Today, this view is unrecognisable, with the buildings demolished and the road a dual carriageway (the A61).

In 1942 Leeds acquired its first significant batch of second-hand trams: 32 four-wheel cars that had been rendered redundant due to conversions in Hull. These became Leeds Nos 446-77 and one of the first to enter service – No 448 (ex-Hull No 130) – is pictured at the Hunslet terminus. This view was taken during World War II and shows to good effect the impact of war on transport operators. The tram is painted in the wartime khaki livery (which it retained until 1946), the windows are fitted with anti-blast mesh, the headlamp is equipped with a shield in order to reduce glare and the collision fenders are painted white in order to improve visibility during the blackout. Another wartime measure to improve visibility in the blackout can be seen in the background; this was the painting of white bands on the traction columns. The ex-Hull cars were destined to have a relatively short career in Leeds; these 32, plus a further 10 acquired in 1945, were all withdrawn by 1951. The ex-Hull cars were nicknamed 'Kipperboxes' in the West Riding. One of the type – Leeds No 446 (ex-Hull No 132) – was preserved and is now on display in its home city.

In late 1939, Leeds Corporation acquired three ex-London Transport 'HR/2' cars that had been made redundant as a result of the tramway conversion programme in the metropolis prior to World War II. The trio – Nos 277-79 – all dated originally to 1930 and were built by Hurst Nelson of Motherwell on EMB bogies. Leeds was interested in the purchase of further trams of this type from London but the outbreak of war in September 1939 and the inevitable delay to the planned conversion of the surviving routes in London meant that no further 'HR/2s' were available. No 279 was the last of the trio to enter service – in July 1940 – but was stored between August 1945 and June 1946 as its bogies and controllers were temporarily fitted to the ex-Sunderland single-deck car No 288 (the car that was subsequently rebuilt as No 600).

No 279 is seen here at the Hunslet terminus in April 1954 shortly after it was fitted with single blind indicators. Hunslet was originally a short working on the longer route to Rothwell; beyond the city boundary at Thwaite Gate the track was owned by the Yorkshire (West Riding) Electric Tramways Co Ltd and the company operated services through to Wakefield. The Rothwell route, although on company-owned track, was largely operated by the corporation. The company-owned section beyond Thwaite Gate was converted to bus operation in May 1932 but the Hunslet service itself was to survive until conversion on 18 April 1959. By that date, No 279 was also history; it was finally withdrawn in September 1957.

The Hunslet route was latterly the regular haunt of the three single-deck cars constructed in the early 1950s as prototypes for the proposed subway scheme. No 600 had originally been Sunderland No 85; this single-deck car had been built by Brush in 1931 on the same manufacturer's maximum-traction bogies for use on the Villette Road route. Stored at the start of World War II, the tram was sold to Leeds – as No 288 from 1948 – in November 1944 but, despite testing over a period of time, did not enter passenger service. However, work on its reconstruction took place periodically from 1949 onwards and, following the acquisition of two EMB bogies from Liverpool Corporation (salvaged from trams destroyed in the Green Lane depot fire), the rebuilt car was first tested in early 1953 but it was not until August 1954 that the car finally entered service. Seen here in April 1955, the tram was destined for a short life, being withdrawn in September 1957. Stored thereafter, the tram was preserved in 1960 and is now based at the National Tramway Museum.

YORK ROAD ROUTES

Until 7 April 1939, when the track along York Street was doubled, outbound trams operated along York Street whilst inbound trams operated via Marsh Lane and Kirkgate. Thereafter, inbound cars travelled along York Street before using Harper Street to gain access to Kirkgate. Although the existing route along Marsh Lane survived as a diversionary route – and was used as such during 1942 when the track on Harper Street was repaired – it was officially closed on 19 November 1944. Here No 538 – previously London Transport No 2094 – can be seen turning into Kirkgate from Harper Street with an inbound service on route 20 from Halton.

Heading inbound along York Street past the Central Bus Station is 'Horsfield' No 171 as AEC Regent V with a Roe H33/27R body No 801 heads outbound on route 15 towards Seacroft South Parkway. The section along York Street was used solely by outbound trams until the track was doubled in 1939; inbound cars headed along Marsh Lane and KIrkgate. Although undated, this view must date to after 21 July 1956 as the existing tram service 15 to Whingate was converted to bus operation that day with services being extended eastwards to Seacroft; No 801 was also new that year. The Central Bus Station opened in 1938; refurbished in 1964, the site was rebuilt and officially reopened in March 1996. The architecture of the original bus station echoed that of the Quarry Hill flats, part of which can be seen on the extreme left of the photograph.

This project, largely completed in the late 1930s (but not finished until 1941), included 938 flats over a 36-acre site and provided accommodation for some 3,000 people. Built using a prefabricated method with steel frames and precast concrete, the flats suffered from a number of problems and were demolished in the late 1970s.

With evidence of work in progress on the outbound track, one of the ex-London Transport 'Feltham' cars – No 560 – heads inbound along York Road at its junction with Dawlish Avenue.

No 560 was one of the 'Felthams' that had originally been supplied to London United Tramways; whilst all 50 of the ex-Metropolitan Electric Tramways 'Felthams' that were sold

to Leeds entered service, the GEC-equipped ex-LUT cars were later to arrive and a significant number never re-entered service. No 560 entered service in the West Riding in January 1952 but was destined for only a short second career: it was withdrawn in February 1957. The line heading to the north, visible from the junction in the foreground, was one of the link lines constructed in the 1930s to serve the new Torre Road depot (this opened on 8 April 1937 and accommodated trams until 19 November 1955). Although the road has been considerably upgraded since this view was taken – the section occupied by the tramway at this point now forms the approaches to the flyover at the Ivy Street intersection – the terraces of houses on the south side of York Road remain intact.

The main junction, known as Halton Dial, for the trams along York Road was at the Selby Road intersection, where the trams to Cross Gates continued along the main York Road whilst the services to Halton and Temple Newsam headed south-eastwards along Selby Road. Pictured at the crossover just to the west of the junction is 'Feltham' No 501, which was the first of these ex-London trams to reach Leeds, on 1 November 1959. By this date route 26 had ceased to be a tram route and so the tram is presumably on an enthusiasts' tour – one of many that operated during the last weeks of the system. Pictured on the extreme right emerging from Selby Road is a 'Horsfield' from either Halton or Temple Newsam.

The junction for the routes to Halton and Temple Newsam on York Road was at Selby Road, where the Cross Gates service headed east along the main road whilst the other two headed south-east along Selby Road. Pictured heading into Selby Road at the junction is No 525; this was one of 90 bogie cars acquired from London Transport between 1949 and 1951. Nos 501-90 had originally been built by the Feltham-based United Construction Co on bogies supplied by the Electro-Mechanical Brake Co Ltd of West Bromwich during 1930 and 1931; this had originally been Metropolitan Electric Tramways No 339 and, from July 1933, London Passenger Transport Board No 2083. The tram operated in Leeds between March 1951 and the end of the system in November 1959. The intersection between the A64 (York Road) and Selby Road is still one of the primary junctions on this important arterial road but the view here – apart from the addition of traffic lights – is still recognisable.

In 1909 part of the Temple Newsam estate was compulsorily purchased by Leeds Corporation for the construction of a new sewage Road Works. Shortly after World War I, in 1922, the then owner of the Jacobean mansion and remaining estate, Edward Wood, sold the property to the corporation as a country park and museum. In order to allow easy access for its citizens to the new facilities, a tramway was constructed from the existing Halton route via Temple Newsam Road and a private right of way to the Sylvan terminus, illustrated here. The extension opened in two stages during April 1924. Seen at the terminus is 'Feltham' No 523. This tram had been new as Metropolitan Electric Tramways No 352 before becoming London Passenger Transport Board No 2096 in July 1933. Entering service in Leeds in September 1951, it was one of the batch to survive until the final conversion of the Leeds system in November 1959.

The Halton route originally opened to a terminus on Chapel Street on 30 April 1915; as part of the modernisation of the tramways during the 1930s, the route was doubled and the terminus was relocated to the Irwin Arms on 8 November 1936. It is at this terminus that 'Chamberlain' No 126 is pictured in August 1951. The car, which had been built originally in February 1927, was one of those fitted – in June 1946 – with a replacement Peckham P35 truck. When recorded here, the car still retained its original three-blind destination display; this was modified to a single blind in September 1952. No 126 survived in service until January 1956 and was scrapped the following month. The Halton service was one of those that was to be converted to bus on the last day of tram operation – 7 November 1959.

CROSS GATES

The extension from Killingbeck to Cross Gates opened on 23 September 1924 and pictured at the terminus is 'Feltham' No 517. When entering service in Leeds during January 1951, No 517 – which had been London Transport No 2118 – was equipped with a pantograph, as shown here, and a further three trams – Nos 528-30 – were also so equipped when re-entering service during March and April 1951. However, the experimental use of pantographs was ended when, on 18 May 1951, No 517 brought down the overhead at the junction of Wellington Street and City Square, with the pantograph itself being catapulted onto the roof of the Majestic Cinema. The problem was that the pantograph, being centrally located, could not cope with overhead aligned for the rear-facing bow collectors. This tram was once recorded as travelling at 57mph at Belle Isle Road.

One of the ex-London United Tramways 'Felthams' stands at the terminus at Cross Gates. The concrete shelter was completed in the early 1950s. Although undated, this view predates 21 July 1956 as the route to New Inn from the city centre was converted to bus operation then; after this date, those trams heading inbound from Cross Gates that were not due to terminate in the centre continued through towards Middleton. This ceased on 28 March 1959 with the conversion of routes 12 and 26; thereafter, until final closure, trams terminated in the city centre.

GIPTON

During the interwar years, Leeds Corporation constructed a number of sizeable housing estates in the suburbs, including that at Seacroft to the east. There were a number of proposed tramways to serve the estate but the only section to be completed was the route to Gipton, which opened on 11 September 1936. The route left York Road and headed north-eastwards along Gipton Approach to its terminus.

The terminus was reached via a steep descent – nicknamed Gipton Gulch – and, in April 1954, 'Chamberlain' No 78 can be seen ascending the gradient with a service on route 9 towards Dewsbury Road. No 78 was new in July 1926; originally fitted with a Pivotal four-wheel truck supplied by the Electro-Mechanical Brake Co Ltd of West Bromwich, this was one of the type subsequently – in January 1949 – to be re-equipped with

a Peckham P35 four-wheel truck. No 78 was to be withdrawn from service in July 1956. The central reservation over which the trams operated is still extant, although the distinctive gully has been filled, with the houses on the right having been demolished to permit road improvements. The once verdant fields in the background have also disappeared with the construction of apartment blocks.

On 8 June 1951 'Chamberlain' No 52 is seen at the Gipton terminus, which was located at the junction of Gipton Approach and Wykebeck Valley Road. Powers were obtained – but never exercised – for an extension from here to the York Road end of South Parkway.

When opened in 1936, outbound trams to Gipton carried the route number 21; following the conversion of the Harehills via Beckett Street service on 24 August 1946, the route number 11 was reallocated to the Gipton route on 8 September 1946. The Gipton service

was converted to bus operation on 23 April 1957. No 52 was new originally in March 1927; when recorded here, it was approaching the end of its career as it was withdrawn in September 1951 and scrapped the following month.

COMPTON ROAD

This view taken looking towards the south-west portrays three trams at the intersection of Harehills Road, Beckett Street and Stanley Road. In the distance No 227 – one of 101 open-top four-wheel cars supplied by the Electric Railway & Tramway Carriage Works, Nos 182-282, that were fitted with open-balcony top covers between 1905 and 1909 – is heading towards

Stanley Road depot. On the left, sister car No 212 in open-top form is waiting to access the single-track section down Beckett Street with a service from Compton Road whilst No 137 – one of the Brush-built cars of 1899, has just arrived up Beckett Street, its destination. At this stage the Compton Road trams used Beckett Street; a direct link south from Compton Street

via Stony Rock Lane opened on 5 December 1916, leaving the track in Stanley Road merely to serve the depot (which closed on 13 June 1939). The track along Beckett Street, with its sections of single track, and Harehills Road, route 11 when service numbers were allocated, were abandoned when the service was converted to bus operation on 24 August 1946.

Seen at the Compton Road terminus prior to departing with a service on route 9 to Dewsbury Road is 'Chamberlain' No 425. This was one of 35 cars – Nos 411-45 – that were built at Kirkstall Road Works between 1926 and 1928 and, when new, were fitted with EMB Pivotal four-wheel trucks. This tram, when taken out of service following the conversion of the Compton Road route on 3 April 1954, was the last in operation with its Pivotal truck; as a result, there was an attempt to secure it for preservation. The plan, however, failed, as – in an era before the establishing of the museum at Crich – no accommodation for the tram could be secured. Situated at the Compton Road terminus was the Burton clothing factory and a single-track direct route via Nippet Lane and Stony Rock Lane was opened in 1916; prior to that date, Compton Road trams had operated via Beckett Street and Stanley Road. The track was doubled in 1942, during World War II, to cater for increased traffic to and from the factory and for a possible – never completed – extension towards Seacroft.

Having just turned into Roundhay Road, one of the three ex-London Transport 'HR/2' cars – No 278 – passes Cross Wingham Street, Sheepscar as it heads towards Meanwood and Roundhay. The route up Roundhay Road from its junction with Chapeltown Road opened as a horse tramway in February 1890. From May 1891 steam trams took over operation until, on 29 October 1891, the pioneering electric trams of the Roundhay Electric Tramways were introduced to the Sheepscar to Roundhay section. These were briefly to cease on 31 July 1896, but were reintroduced, following the corporation's takeover, on 2 August 1897. The Moortown via Sheepscar and Roundhay service was to be converted to bus operation on 28 March 1959.

In this view, taken in August 1951, No 278 looks in fine external condition, having recently been repainted into the then new red and cream livery. It had originally been London Passenger Transport Board No 1883 and had entered service in Leeds during December 1939; it was to be withdrawn in September 1957. Although both Roundhay Road and Cross Wingham Street are still extant, all the buildings to the right of the tram have been swept away.

The last brand-new double-deck tram constructed for operation in Leeds was No 276; this was completed at Kirkstall Road Works in 1948 on a Peckham P35 four-wheel truck. Designed as the prototype for a new class of cars, no further examples were constructed. When completed, the car had a three-blind destination display; this view seems to record the tram in an intermediate stage, with the lower half of the upper blind being blanked off. Based at Headingley depot when new, No 276 was regularly used on the Roundhay loop services. In December 1953 the tram re-emerged with only a single-blind destination display. No 276 suffered an electrical fire on 2 September 1957; although some repair work was undertaken, the car was withdrawn and scrapped the following month. The tram is pictured here on the short spur along Stainbeck Lane; this short section was opened on 7 July 1948 and permitted the cars operating on the Chapeltown short working to be diverted to this point from their original terminus at the Queen's Arms. The Briggate to Moortown service via Chapeltown was converted to bus operation on 28 September 1957.

Following on from the construction of the 'Middleton Bogie' cars, the general manager, Vane Moreland, obtained permission to construct a four-wheel version for use on routes with sharper curves. The result was Nos 272-74 that were nicknamed 'Lance Corporals' as a result of their distinctive single V-shaped white band – as demonstrated in this view of No 274, pictured at the junction of Stainbeck Lane and Harrogate Road.

The three cars, completed at Kirkstall Road Works on Maley & Taunton swinglink trucks in 1935, were based at Headingley depot for much of their career, until that depot closed (when they were transferred to Swinegate), and operated almost exclusively on the Roundhay loop services. The cars were built to placate residents on these services who demanded new trams after the introduction of the bogie cars

to the Middleton route. Deemed to be non-standard, the three cars were all withdrawn during 1954 and 1955 and scrapped at the end of 1955. The tracks seen curving towards the west in front of the tram were those opened in 1948 to serve the short Stainbeck Lane spur. Of the buildings visible, only one – the Yorkshire Penny Bank building – is still extant. This dated originally to the late 1930s and survives now as a coffee shop.

Although Leeds had acquired a small number of second-hand trams both before and during World War II, it was after the war that the corporation took advantage of tramway abandonments elsewhere to supplement its fleet and to replace older trams. One of the sources of these second-hand trams was Southampton, where the final services were converted to bus operation on 31 December 1949. In all, Leeds acquired almost 40 redundant trams from the south coast between May 1949 and July 1950; however,

only 11 – Nos 290-300 – actually entered service. Of the remainder, a number were transported to the West Riding but scrapped without entering service whilst others were disposed of in Southampton without ever making the journey north. No 291 – seen here at the crossover at the junction of Allerton Avenue and Street Lane in Moortown on 4 June 1951 – had originally been Southampton No 109 and was new in 1930. Fitted with a Peckham P35 truck, the tram was the last new car acquired by

Southampton. Sold to Leeds in May 1949, it re-entered service in August the same year. The ex-Southampton cars were destined to have a relatively short life in Leeds, with No 291 being the first to be withdrawn (in May 1952). The distinctive shape of the roof was the consequence of creating a fully-enclosed tram capable of passing through the low Bargate in Southampton. A similar tram – No 11 (which was not one of those sold to Leeds) – is currently under restoration in its home city.

One of 50 open-top cars supplied by Brush in 1902 that were subsequently fitted with open-balcony top covers - No 48 – is pictured at Oakwood in about 1915. Visible to the right of the tram is the turning circle used historically by the steam trams; the redundant track was removed during World War I. The ornate building on the right-hand side, which was one of the entrances to Roundhay Park, served as a tramway waiting room and provided toilet facilities. It was built in 1889 and was demolished in 1937.

In April 1955 'Chamberlain No 434 heads inbound along the side reservation on Princes Avenue as it approaches Roundhay Road in Oakwood. Today, this view – albeit without the trams – is still remarkably similar, although vegetation has become much more verdant on the traffic island and the area occupied by the tram track is now used for parking. The clock tower dated originally to 1904 and was built by the local firm of William Potts & Sons Ltd to the design of Leeming & Leeming. It was originally planned that the clock would be a feature of the rebuilt Kirkgate Market in the city, but a change of plans resulted in it becoming unsuitable and so it ended up being erected at Oakwood. The tower underwent a major restoration in 2015. No 434 was new in April 1928 and was to receive a replacement Peckham P35 four-wheel truck in August 1948; it survived in service until June 1955.

Pictured running through the roundabout at the intersection of Roundhay Road and Easterly Road with an inbound service heading towards Haddon Place, on the Kirkstall Road route, is No 151. This was the first of four cars – Nos 151-54 – constructed at Kirkstall Road Works in 1930 that were the prototypes for the 100-strong 'Horsfield' type. Of the four, all bar No 153 were fitted with Peckham P35 four-wheel trucks whilst No 153 received an EMB flexible truck (No 151 was initially fitted with a Smith pendulum truck but was soon replaced). No 151 was withdrawn in March 1959 and scrapped three months later. The Haddon Place short working was abandoned on 7 March 1954 with all service cars that had terminated there being extended to the Abbey itself until the service was converted to bus operation on 3 April 1954. Visible heading out to the east along Eastlerly Road is the overhead for the short spur constructed in 1940. Today, this view of the road junction is radically different; the roundabout has been dispensed with in favour of a complex junction with traffic lights; the Yorkshire Penny Bank branch building is still extant – albeit no longer a bank – and the terrace of shops on the west side of Roundhay Road also still survives.

CREDITS

Lost Tramways of England – Leeds East
Published in Great Britain in 2021
by Graffeg Limited.

Written by Peter Waller copyright © 2021.
Designed and produced by Graffeg Limited
copyright © 2021.

Graffeg Limited, 24 Stradey Park Business
Centre, Mwrwg Road, Llangennech, Llanelli,
Carmarthenshire, SA14 8YP, Wales, UK.
Tel: 01554 824000. www.graffeg.com.

Peter Waller is hereby identified as the author
of this work in accordance with section 77 of
the Copyrights, Designs and Patents Act 1988.

A CIP Catalogue record for this book is
available from the British Library.

ISBN 9781914079580

1 2 3 4 5 6 7 8 9

MIX
Paper from
responsible sources
FSC® C014138

Photo credits

© John Meredith/Online Transport Archive:
pages 14, 20, 22, 30. © Julian Thompson/
Online Transport Archive: pages 15, 52, 60.
© Harry Luff/Online Transport Archive: pages
16. © F. E. J. Ward/Online Transport Archive:
pages 17, 31, 35, 41, 43, 46. © Phil Tatt/
Online Transport Archive: pages 18, 27, 28, 39,
40, 47, 48, 51, 56, 62. © Maurice O'Connor/
National Tramway Museum: page 19. © R.
W. A. Jones/Online Transport Archive: pages
25, 32, 55, 58, 59, 63. © J. H. Roberts/Online
Transport Archive: page 29. © W. A. Camwell/
National Tramway Museum: page 33. © A.
Brooks Collection/Online Transport Archive:
page 37. © J. Joyce/Online Transport Archive:
pages 44, 49. © F. K. Farrell Collection/Online
Transport Archive: page 45. © Keith Carter
Online Transport Archive: page 50. © Barry
Cross Collection/Online Transport Archive:
page 53. © Leeds City Tramways/Barry Cross
Collection/Online Transport Archive: page 61.

The photographs used in this book have come
from a variety of sources. Wherever possible
contributors have been identified although
some images may have been used without
credit or acknowledgement and if this is the
case apologies are offered and full credit will
be given in any future edition.

Cover: York Street.
Back cover: Hunslet Lane, Hunslet route,
Permanent Way Yard.

Lost Tramways of Wales:

- **Cardiff** ISBN 9781912213122
- **North Wales** ISBN 9781912213139
- **South Wales and Valleys**
  ISBN 9781912213146
- **Swansea and Mumbles**
  ISBN 9781912213153

Lost Tramways of England:

- **Birmingham North** ISBN 9781912654390
- **Birmingham South** ISBN 9781912654383
- **Bradford** ISBN 9781912654406
- **Brighton** ISBN 9781912654376
- **Bristol** ISBN 9781912654345
- **Coventry** ISBN 9781912654338
- **Leeds West** ISBN 9781913733506
- **Leeds East** ISBN 9781914079580
- **Nottingham** ISBN 9781912654352
- **Southampton** ISBN 9781912654369

Lost Tramways of Scotland:

- **Aberdeen** ISBN 9781912654413
- **Dundee** ISBN 9781912654420
- **Edinburgh** ISBN 9781913733513
- **Glasgow South** ISBN 9781914079528
- **Glasgow North** ISBN 9781914079542

Lost Tramways of Ireland:

- **Belfast** ISBN 9781914079504